EVERY BIT OF IT

Erin,
Happy Reading!
- K

EVERY BIT OF IT

Katherine Bogden

Winner of the Harriss Poetry Prize
Michael Salcman, Prize Series Editor
Tom Lux, 2012 Contest Judge

CITYLIT
PRESS

Baltimore, Maryland

Library of Congress Control Number: 2012943415

ISBN 978-1-936328-08-6

CityLit Project is a 501(c)(3) Nonprofit Organization

Federal Tax ID Number: 20-0639118

Printed in the United States of America

First Edition

Book Design: Gregg Wilhelm

Cover Art: Stephen Pace (1918–2010)

Woman in a Black Robe, 1962

Oil on canvas

24x18 inches

Collection of Spanierman Gallery, LLC, New York

© Stephen and Palmina Pace Trust

Author Photograph: Roz Akin

CITYLIT
PRESS

c/o CityLit Project

120 S. Curley Street

Baltimore, MD 21224

410.274.5691

www.CityLitProject.org

info@citylitproject.org

Contents

Introduction

One never judges a book by its epigraph, but
the one in this book immediately arrested me.
(It'll probably be on the next page or two.) An
epigraph—a quote from someone else—in a book,
or on an individual poem, is supposed to have an
echo of what's to come next. A hint of its tone or
concerns. It's an apt epigraph for this spare, yet
vivid, little book. The speaker (the I) of these poems
is usually speaking to a "you," or about a "him." It's
a safe bet that the "you/him" is the same person/
character. A reader should never assume that a poem
written in first person singular is autobiographical—
though it is 99% of the time. The "I/you" poem is
ubiquitous in contemporary American poetry.

That's where the similarities between these
poems and most "I/you" poems end. Otherwise,
this book unfurls an emotional life more by what
it artfully withholds, by what it leaves unsaid, yet
makes implicit. These are love poems, but unlike
most love poems, they have just below their surface
a current of tension, of tenderness, of reverberant
mystery. The book begins with a prose-poem and the
speaker is waiting for the beloved to arrive: "… for
in a moment you will arrive, and for that moment,
in no original way, the whole earth will seem as if it
were born, from magma to ocean, for us." It's already
original when the speaker says it's not an original
feeling! That's the first hint of the darker side to these
poems. A few poems later one begins with "Sixteen

black hairs line the sink." The specificity of 16 (who counts?) is what makes that line about more than the quotidian life of a man and a woman sharing a sink. Perhaps my favorite poem is "Untitled (with Croquet)" where fledglings (or are they?) fall from their nests and "shatter" on the sidewalk. Then the I and you are "plump with aimless walks, talk of the weather, /here and there a pick-up game of croquet." Croquet invokes gentility, summer lawns, even affluence. And one plays it with wooden balls and big hammers!

This books reveals, as I've said, by what it hides. Life is often like that. This little book, this sequence of poems, is of a whole, connected; yet each one could stand alone. It tells a deeply human story and tells it slant, as Emily Dickinson said, when, I believe, she was talking about how originality might come about. And that's what these poems are: original. And alive.

Tom Lux
Georgia Institute of Technology
Atlanta, GA

"But this is what the world is like. And I love the world. I long to devour it all, every bit of it. Sometimes this longing makes my heart beat so fast that the next day it hardly beats at all."

—

Boris Pasternak to Marina Tsvetayeva
July 1, 1926

Every Bit of It

Untitled (with Forsythia)

White as milk the vase rests on the counter. Stem by
stem I add the forsythia. Stem by stem—bear with
me—for in a moment you will arrive, and for that
moment, in no original way, the whole earth will
seem as if it were born, from magma to ocean, for us.
We will find it incomprehensible that one day—we
will find it incomprehensible, the possibilities.

After Reading That a Loss of Sea Water Is Causing a Rise in the World's Jellyfish Population

I said, does it hurt still? You said, it does sometimes.
I said, when you touch it

do you find it's worse? Sometimes, you said.
And are you going back

in the water? I have to, you said. I said, I miss you
you're what I think about when people say: regret.

Do you know, you said, that jellyfish cannot swim?
They simply drift with the tide and sting

involuntarily, when they find a warm body.
I didn't know, I said. And you said: now you do.

And when I tried to ask where
we go from here, I found

I was already mouth-deep in salt water
my translucent body pulsing with the sea.

Living with Him

Sixteen black hairs line the sink
he must have left them after shaving.
When I come back into the kitchen
I see him hold a paring knife to an avocado.
Fingers pressed against skin
he makes one slice and twists.
I see him lay it flat against the counter, scoop
the insides with a spoon.

Untitled (with Cicadas)

Every time I touch him I remember.
He is like a string around the finger I can't untie,
unsettling.
Like the sudden disappearance of the cicadas:
one night sighing their songs and
then without warning
the only sound is the neighbors—
and I can't stop wondering what they're doing.

Untitled (with Croquet)

Have you noticed it's happening again?
The fledglings (are they even fledglings?)
falling from their nests, shattering
like glass on the sidewalks.
I know, I know—Spring asks nothing of us.
And isn't it an affable season?
One which undoubtedly will pass as always—
plump with aimless walks, talk of the weather,
here and there a pick-up game of croquet.

Picnic (Prospect Park)

Beneath two budding elms we spread
our blanket, give in

to our legs and reveal
what we've carried:

sweet pickles and hot mustard
sharp cheddar, crackers, wine

in a paper bag, plastic
cups. I watch him, thick hair pushed

behind each ear
uncork the bottle. We're not alone.

The park swells
with other couples, beside us a woman tumbles

over her man, tucks
skirt tight to thigh. They touch

in their own shade.
Somehow I doubt she is thinking of the pears

she left sitting on the counter.

Two A.M.

I can hear them again, the couple
in the apartment above us.
Love, what keeps us here?
Aren't we different? Aren't we
meant for something else?
Do you remember, one night like this
I told you: none of this is private,
not when we live above somebody, below somebody
stacked among floorboards, walls, years of paint.

Who Wants to be Persephone, Anyway

He's gone again, traveling.
The first day the cat and I wander
the apartment in repeat.
She sits in his salvaged chair, wanting.
I can't finish crossword puzzles.
By Wednesday, we adjust: the cat lays
on the newspaper
covering the empty puzzle-boxes.
Does this mean that I don't love him?
Or only that I can live without him?

Untitled (After Argument)

For the rest of the morning I tried to imagine the sky
without the flocking of birds,
the telephone wires relieved of those dark silhouettes

like returning to an unfamiliar house
the newspaper still at the door, crisp in plastic
and inside an empty chair—
where I'd expect to find his coat.

Sunday Repeats

I've watched now for minutes the fruit flies hover
and fall from sight.

The kitchen sink is clogged, I know.
Something flesh-colored and flecked with green

is down there and even poking slightly from the top.
There was a time I might have scooped what's inside

bare-handed, poured Drano down in hope
whatever's blocking might be washed away.

But, it's been a strange summer. So much rain.
And he, he has a new, unexpected haircut.

The day he forgot his keys
I imagined him, when I opened the door, a stranger.

Primitive

Too much wine and here I am, taking the
garbage to the curb, barefoot. Too much rain
and earthworms untuck from their muddy beds,
slink to asphalt. Too much stillness and the
earth throws an owl at the night, with a fist-
curling screech. Too much loneliness—too much
loneliness—and I return to you.

Untitled (with Backgammon)

It's been what? An hour? Maybe two—soon the day
will subside (leaving my skin pink as the cherry-
blossoms) and I'll say look—as the last kites fly over
us—how their tails will shimmer like the skin of a
great golden snake or—we've been drinking wine,
I'm drowsy. It's his move—watch—how he makes it,
slowly, counts each point—while around us, around
our game, the city approaches the hour the white
moths find their lampposts.

Delicate Things

This garden is full
of them: leggy crickets, cotton-topped
dandelions, browned grasses
that arch and bow like goosenecks.
And I know, I know, you and I, we're here—
but really, are we so delicate?
Or are we more like those
other, impenetrable things:
the iron gate, the stiff stone bench?
Look, here they come again, those fat, wet drops—
let's wait here, share this umbrella.
Oh, love, don't you feel it? It's becoming clear.

Rainy Day, Brooklyn

Like a crow the umbrella throws back its wings
black body suddenly boundless.
We run to the apartment,
water drips from everywhere, from the soles
of our unremarkable shoes. We keep the silence,
brush drops from our sleeves.
All those things I've said?
Maybe we're not so different.

Apple Picking

Remember when we walked far into the fields
not because there were better apples

but because there were fewer people?
For a while we didn't see anyone but each other.

Untitled (with Bearskin Rug)

Perhaps I've had too much bourbon
but just now it seems
this bearskin rug could rise
if he wanted.
And how should we great him
you and I, if he does, we who have felt
his course hairs kiss the soles
of our feet?

How Strange

these clumps of dust
are made partly from our skin.
I can't stop thinking,
vacuuming under the couch, the book shelves
that they should look like us
(yours freckled, mine fair)
but there's no resemblance.
And isn't it easier to clean this way—
like eating a fish without its face?

Walking Home on Seventh Avenue, You in Your Burnt Orange Sweater, Humming

I think of other nights
when we keep the silence like this
not because we are full and drowsy,
but because there's so much
we can't bear to say
and don't those nights make this all the sweeter now?

On Taking Your Name

Darling, don't you see Juliet and I are at odds again?
As sweet? Yes, but not the same.
With another name one becomes another
blossom altogether—
and who are we to say what remains?

Can I Trust You

with this secret?
One morning you will go out for milk
and come home to see me
as I truly am: vulnerable and unsure.
And what will happen then, over breakfast,
as our spoons lick the sides
of our cereal bowls,
when you see me as I see myself?

You and I

Remember that humid day when you and I stood
on a Brooklyn-bound F train, two bodies pressed
among bodies, and *écoutez*, a man whispered
écoutez, for an upright bass was playing, desolate and
unpredictable? In that moment I caught a glimpse
of another life, where something followed us home
from that place, tangled with our feet in the sheets
we kicked off—and *écoutez*, it whispered, *écoutez*.
And do you know it entered our quivering tendons,
then, taught us to forgo bone for maple, spruce,
ebony—in another life, my love, we were only music.
We lived above the city in the trees.

Acknowledgments

I am—and will remain—grateful to Tom Lux for selecting this manuscript for the Harriss Poetry Prize. Thank you.

I am grateful also to Gregg Wilhelm and Michael Salcman of CityLit Press.

For inspiration I'd like to acknowledge Jane Kenyon for her lovely translation of Anna Akmatova's poems—*Twenty Poems*; also Anna Akmatova herself.

For their continuous support I thank my friends, family, and my husband, John.

For her precise and patient criticism of many of these poems while I was her student at Sarah Lawrence College, I thank Marie Howe.

Many thanks are also due to *LUMINA* where a version of "Sunday Repeats" first appeared; to *Poor Claudia* where "Untitled (with Forsythia)," "Untitled (with Backgammon)" and "You and I," first appeared; to *Juncture: A Writerly Newspaper* where "Untitled (with Cicadas)" first appeared; to *Washington Square Review* where "After Reading that a Loss of Seawater is Causing a Rise in the Worlds Jellyfish Population" first appeared; and to *Coal City Review* where "Primitive" first appeared.

I remain forever grateful.

About the Poet

Katherine Bogden lives in Brooklyn, New York, where she is an editor at Ugly Duckling Presse. She earned her MFA from Sarah Lawrence College.

Photo: Roz Akin

About CityLit Press

CityLit Press's mission is to provide a venue for writers who might otherwise be overlooked by larger publishers due to the literary nature or regional focus of their projects. It is the imprint of nonprofit CityLit Project, founded in Baltimore in 2004.

CityLit nurtures the culture of literature in Baltimore and throughout Maryland by creating enthusiasm for literature, building a community of avid readers and writers, and opening opportunities for young people and diverse audiences to embrace the literary arts

Thank you to our major supporters: the Maryland State Arts Council, the Baltimore Office of Promotion and The Arts, and the Baltimore Community Foundation. More information and documentation is available at www.guidestar.org.

Additional support is provided by individual contributors. Financial support is vital for sustaining the ongoing work of the organization. Secure, on-line donations can by made at our web site (click on "Donate").

CityLit is a member of the Greater Baltimore Cultural Alliance, the Maryland Association of Nonprofit Organizations, and the Writers' Conferences and Centers division of the Association of Writers and Writing Programs (AWP).

For submission guidelines, information about CityLit Press's poetry chapbook contests, and all the programs and services offered by CityLit, please visit

www.citylitproject.org / CityLit Press / Harriss Prize.

Launched in 2009, the Harriss Poetry Prize is named in honor of Clarinda Harriss, eminent Baltimore poet, publisher, and professor of English at Towson University. Harriss, educated at Johns Hopkins University and Goucher College, is a widely published, award-winning poet and she serves as editor/director of BrickHouse Books, Maryland's oldest literary press.

2012 Judge: Tom Lux
2011 Judge: Dick Allen
2010 Judge: Michael Salcman

For complete guidelines, please go to www. citylitproject.org and click on "CityLit Press." Send entry fee, manuscript with table of contents, acknowledgments, and two coversheets (one with name, title, mailing address, daytime phone, and email address and one with *title only*) to:

Harriss Poetry Prize
CityLit Press
c/o CityLit Project
120 S. Curley Street
Baltimore, MD 21224

Submission deadline is October 1 (postmarked).